Vintage Bird Coloring Book for Adults
Relaxation with 30 Coloring Pages of Audubon's Birds of America

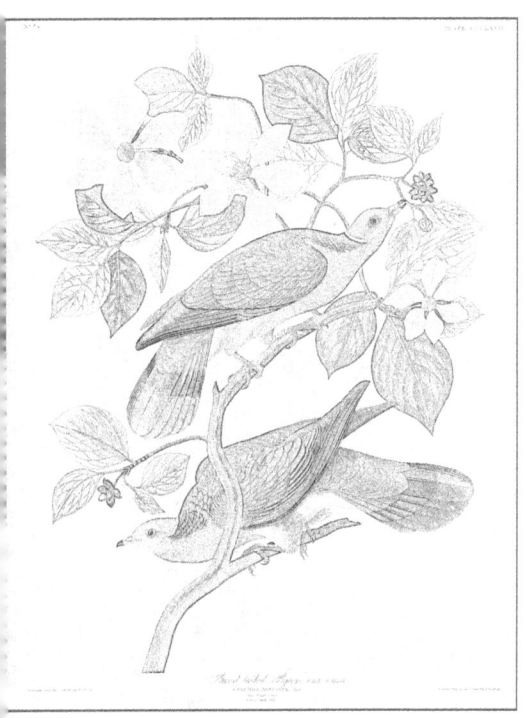
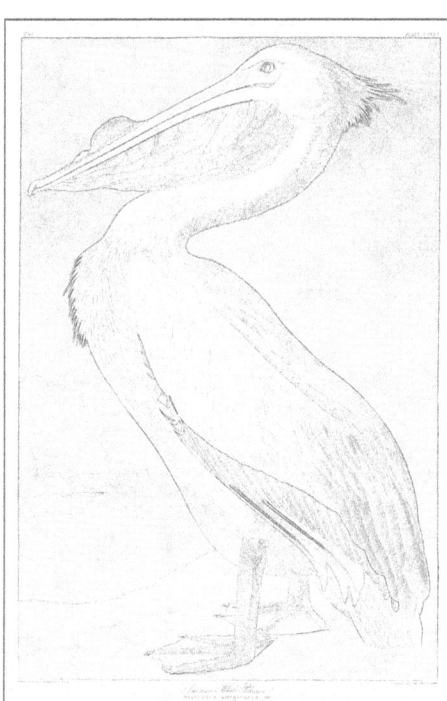
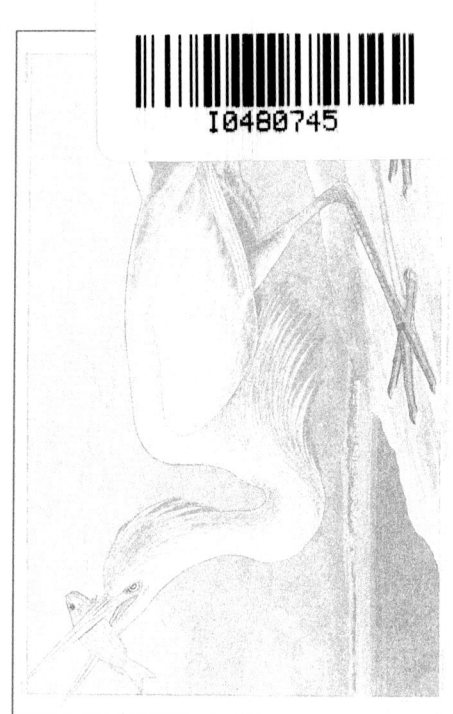
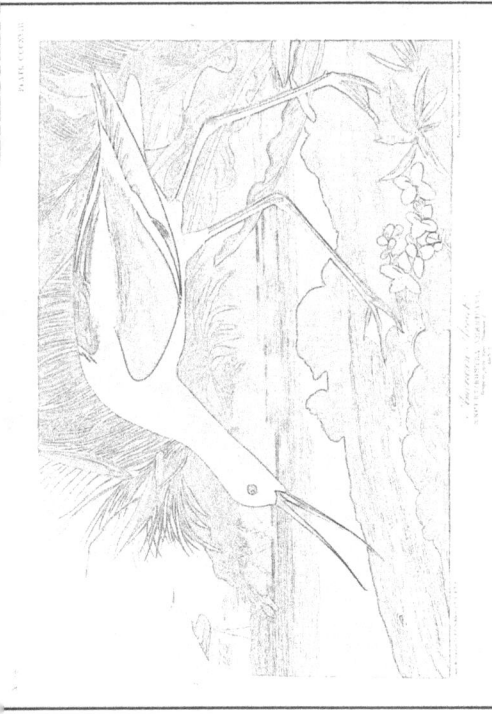
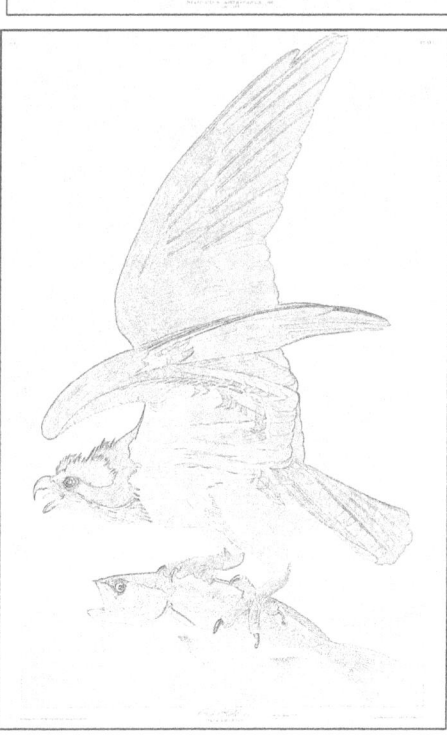
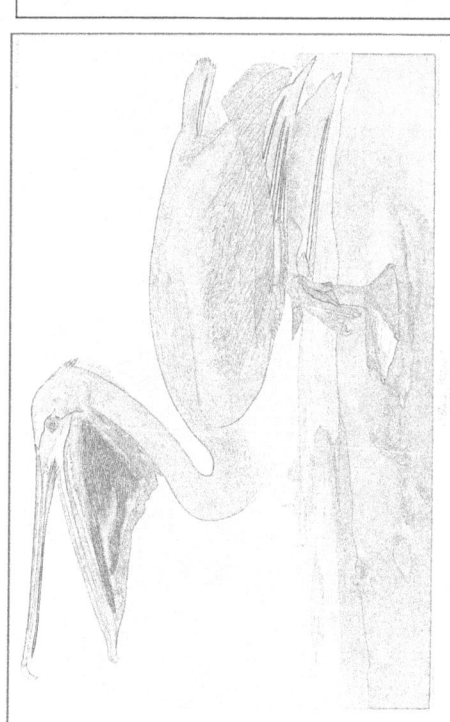

Ada Ashley

PLATE CCCLXVII.

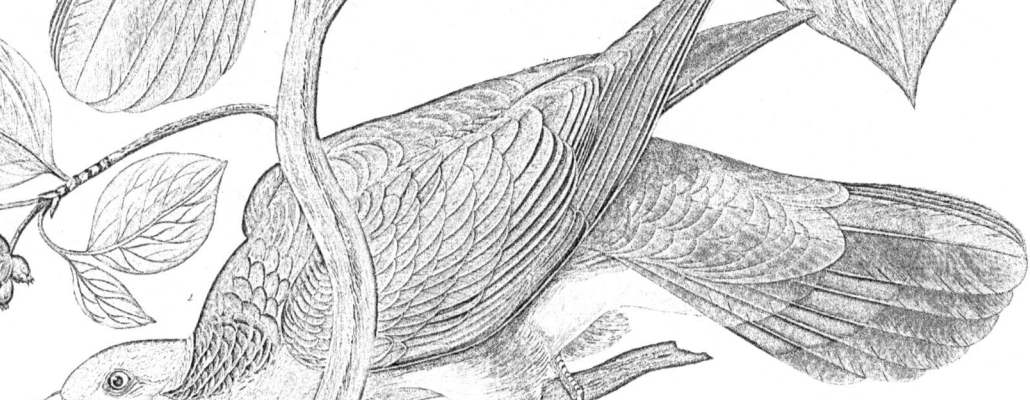

Band-tailed Pigeon. 1. Male. 2. Female.
COLUMBA FASCIATA, Say.
Plant Small Cornel.
Genus Nuttalli. Aud.

Drawn from Nature by J. J. Audubon, F.R.S. F.L.S.
Engraved, Printed and Coloured by R. Havell 1837.

PLATE. CCCXI

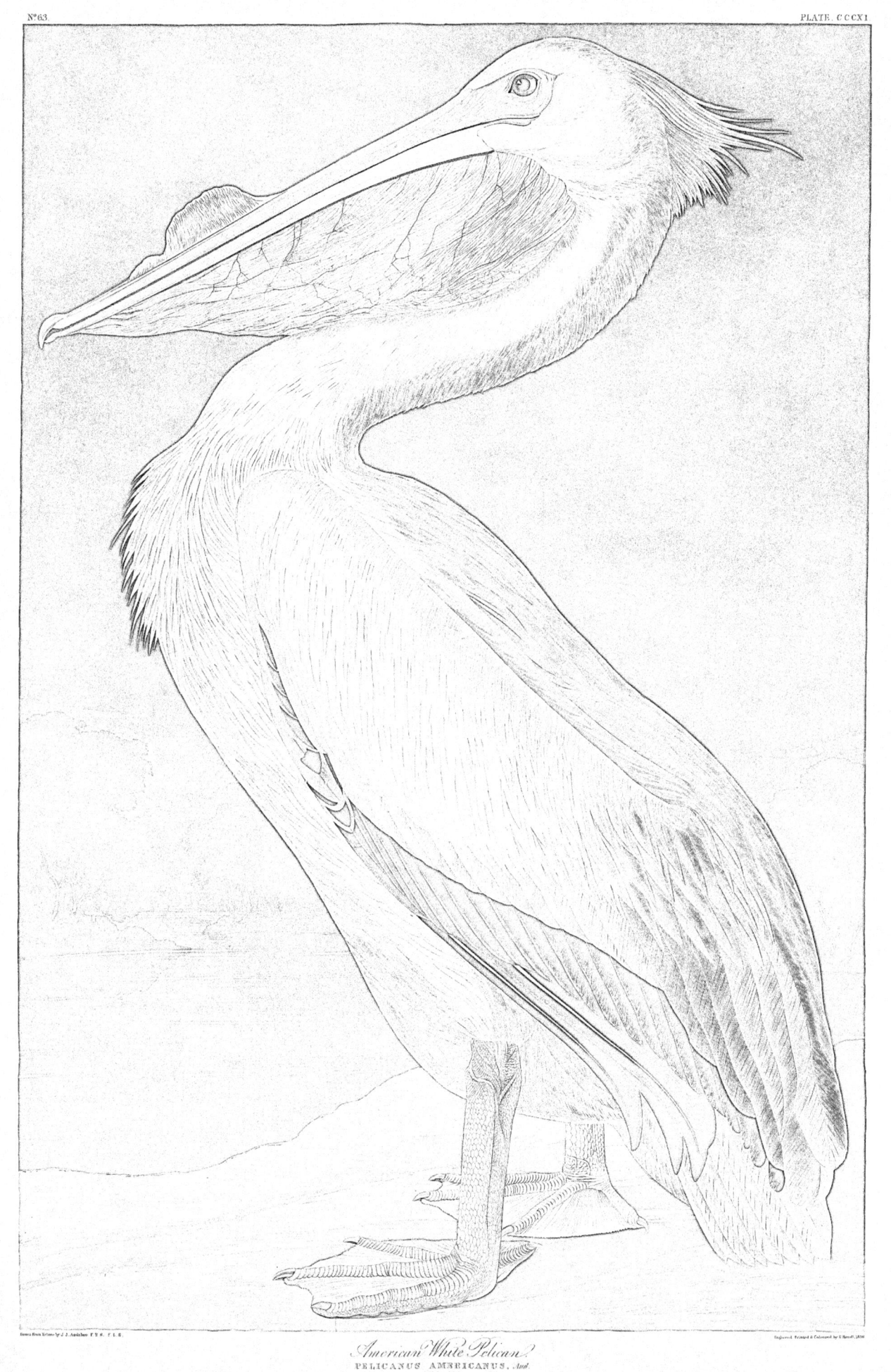

Drawn from Nature by J. J. Audubon F.R.S. F.L.S.

Engraved, Printed & Coloured by R Havell 1836.

American White Pelican

PELICANUS AMERICANUS, Aud.

Male Adult.

PLATE CCLXXXI

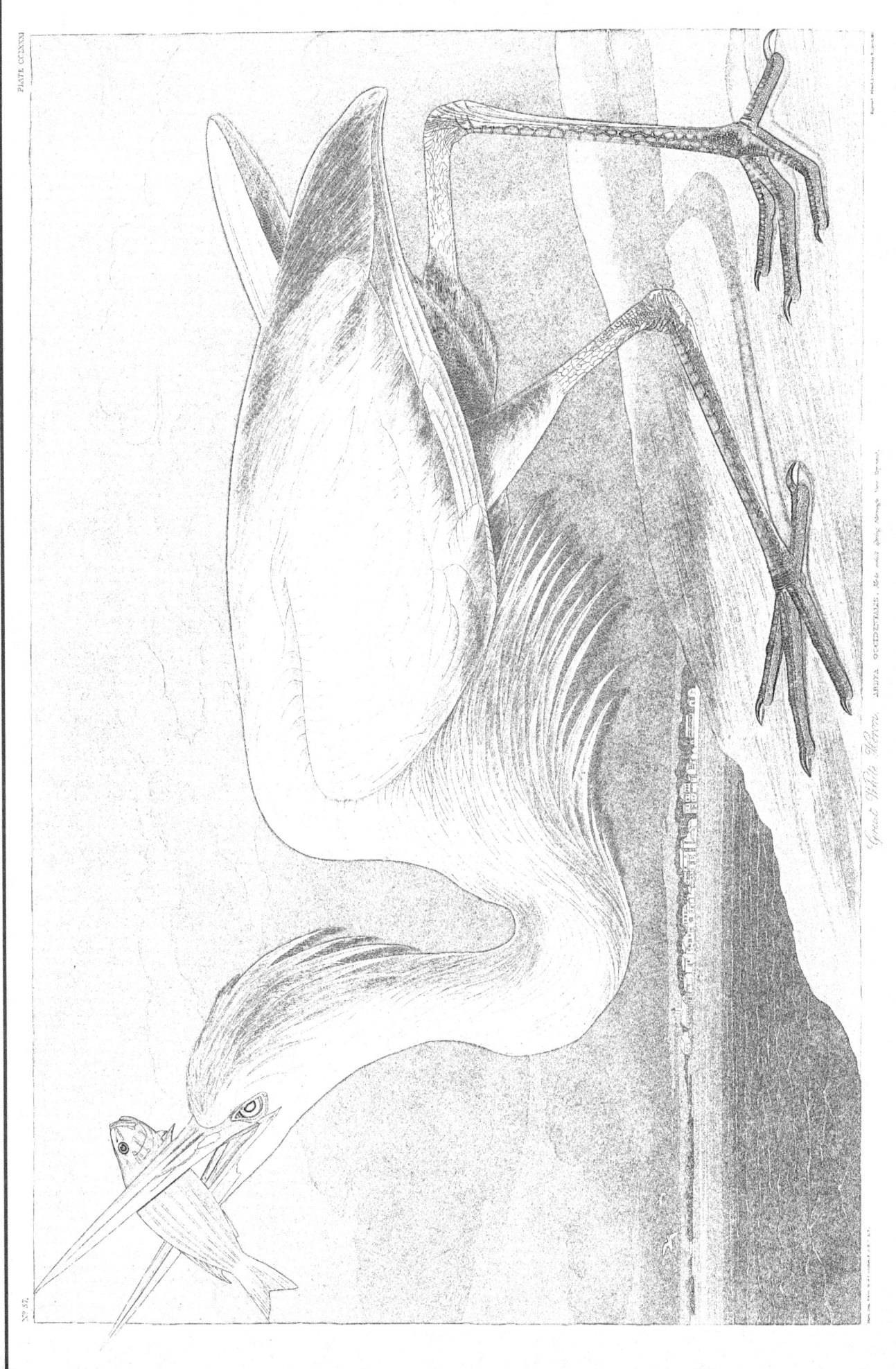

Great White Heron.
ARDEA OCCIDENTALIS. *Nat. size. from Nature.*

PLATE CCCXVII

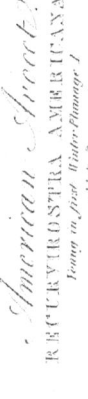

American Avocet?
RECURVIROSTRA AMERICANA,
Young in first Winter Plumage 1
Adult 2

Drawn from Nature by J. J. Audubon, F. R. S. F. L. S

Engraved, Printed and Coloured by R. Havell 1836.

PLATE III

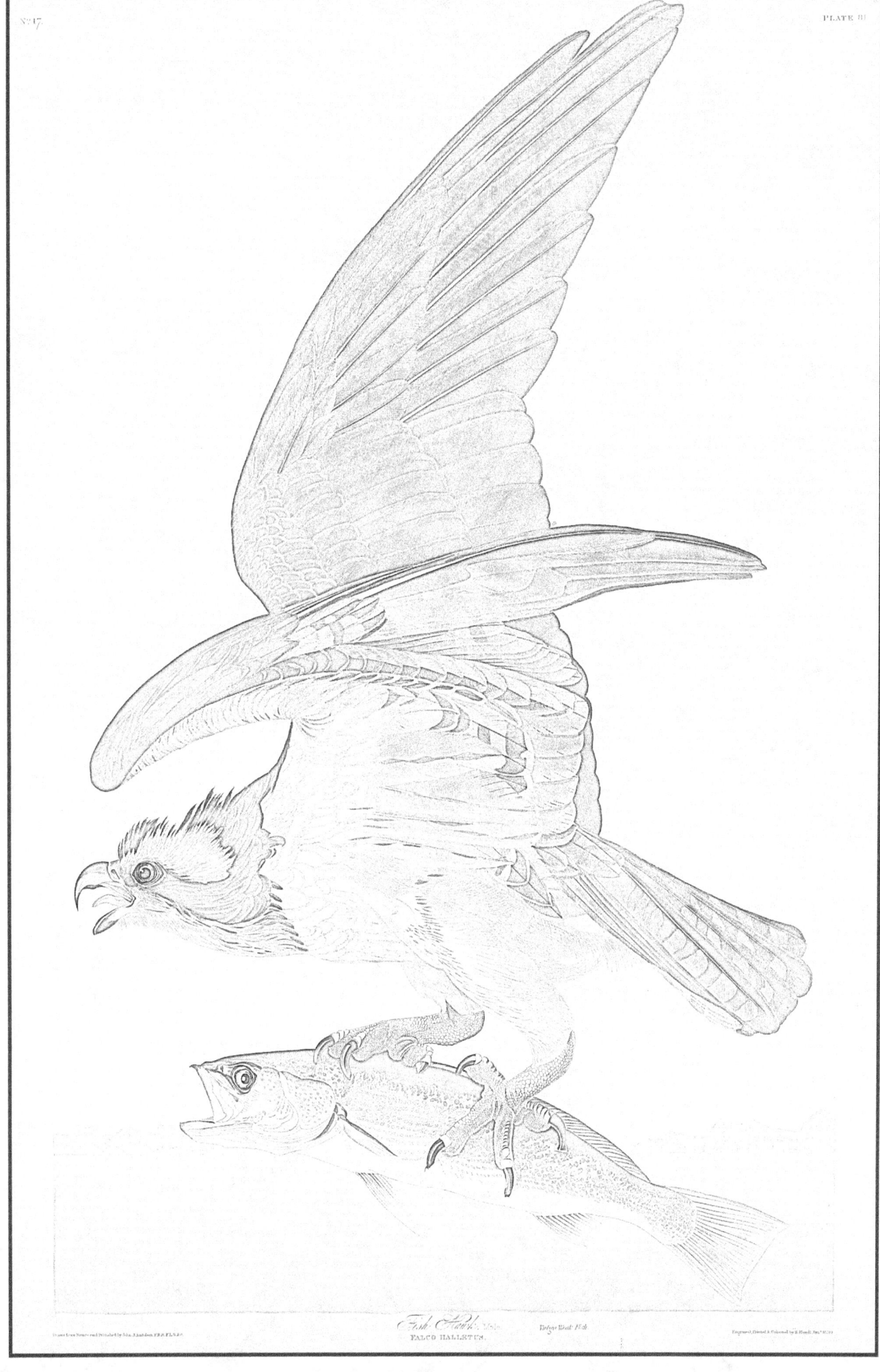

Fish Hawk, Male.   Weak Fish.
FALCO HALIÆTUS.

Drawn from Nature and Published by John J. Audubon, F.R.S. F.L.S. &c.

Engraved, Printed & Coloured by R. Havell, Sen.r & Jun.r

PLATE CCCXXI

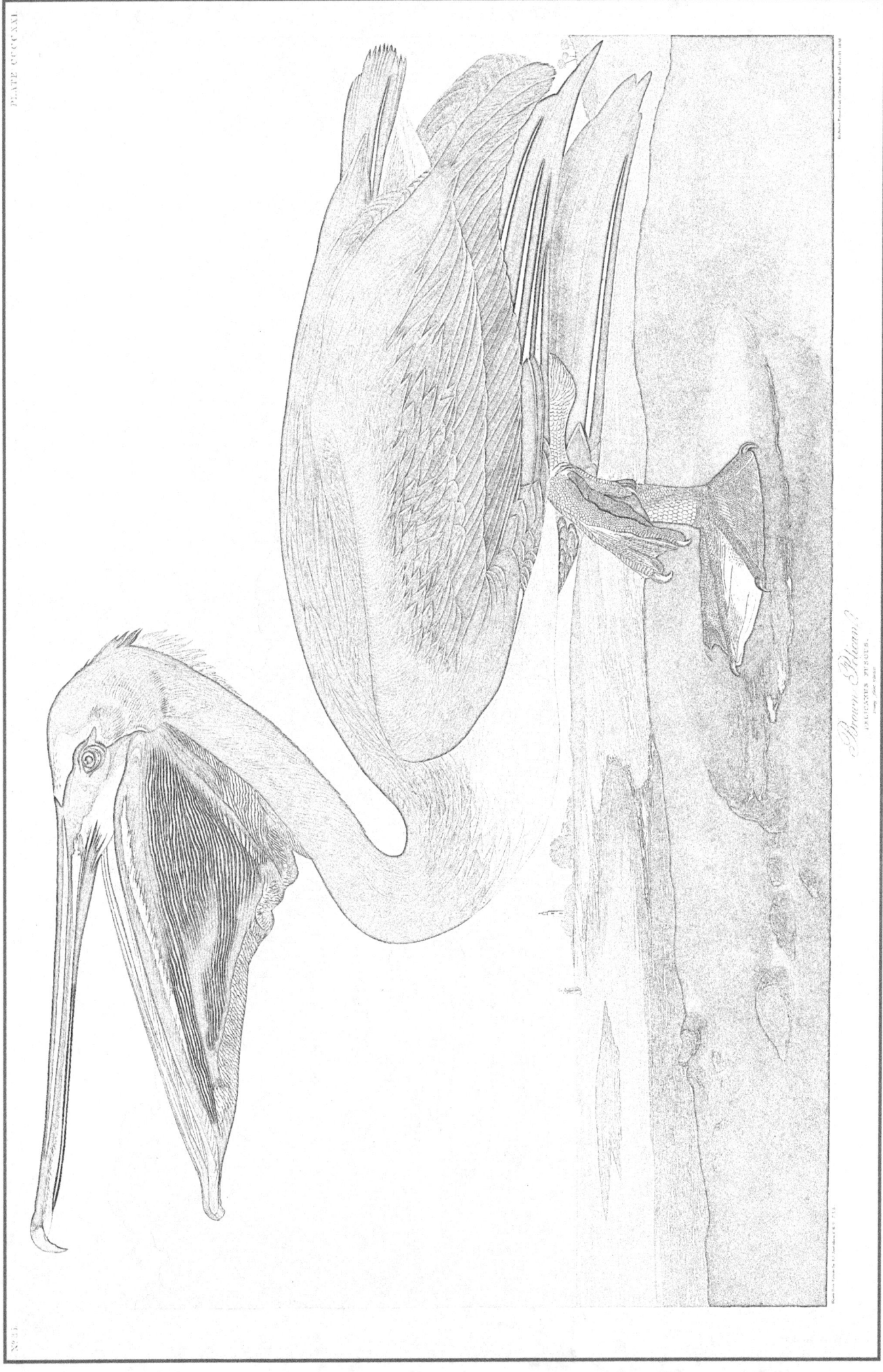

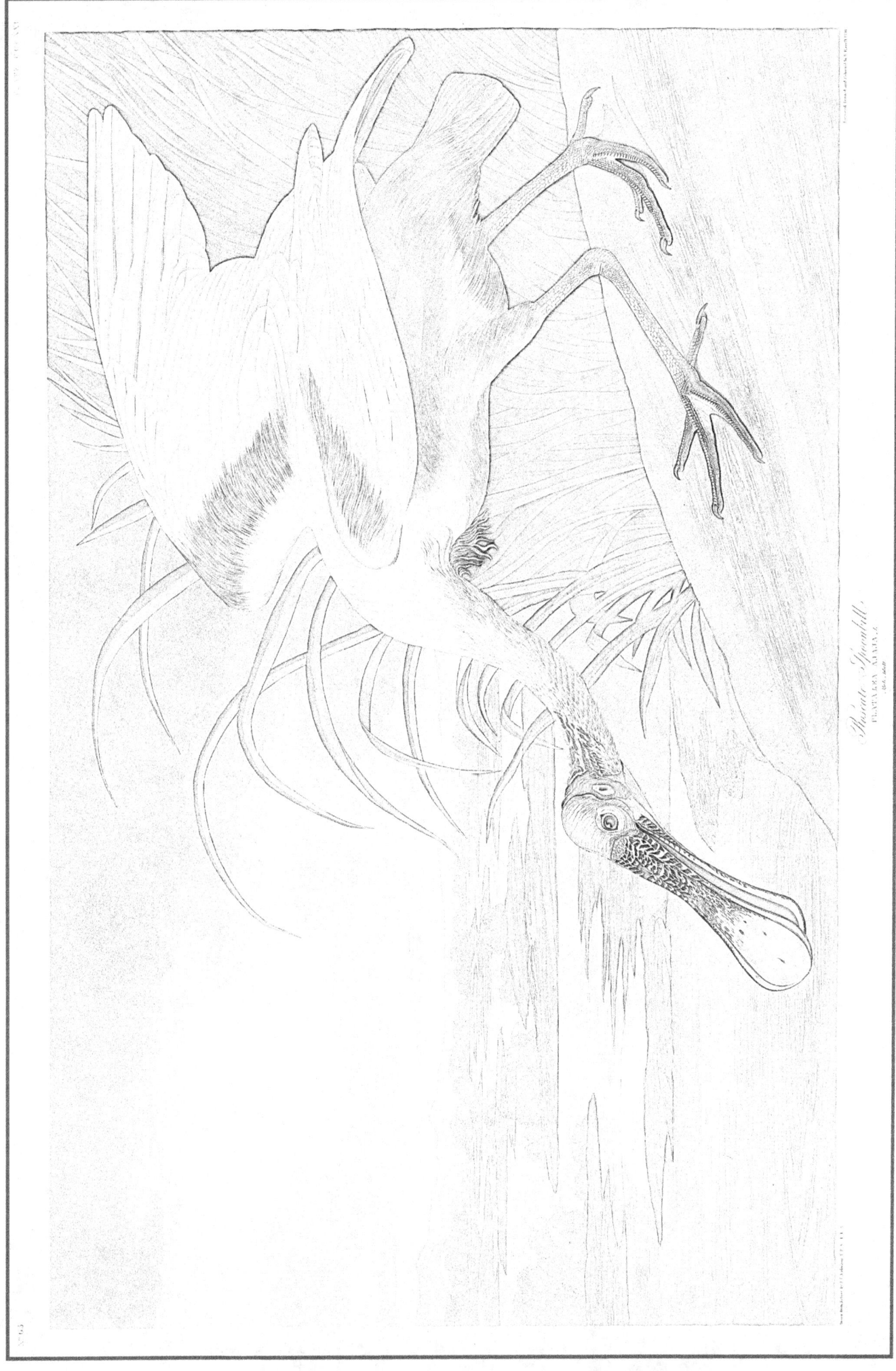

PLATE CCXXIII

N°. 45.

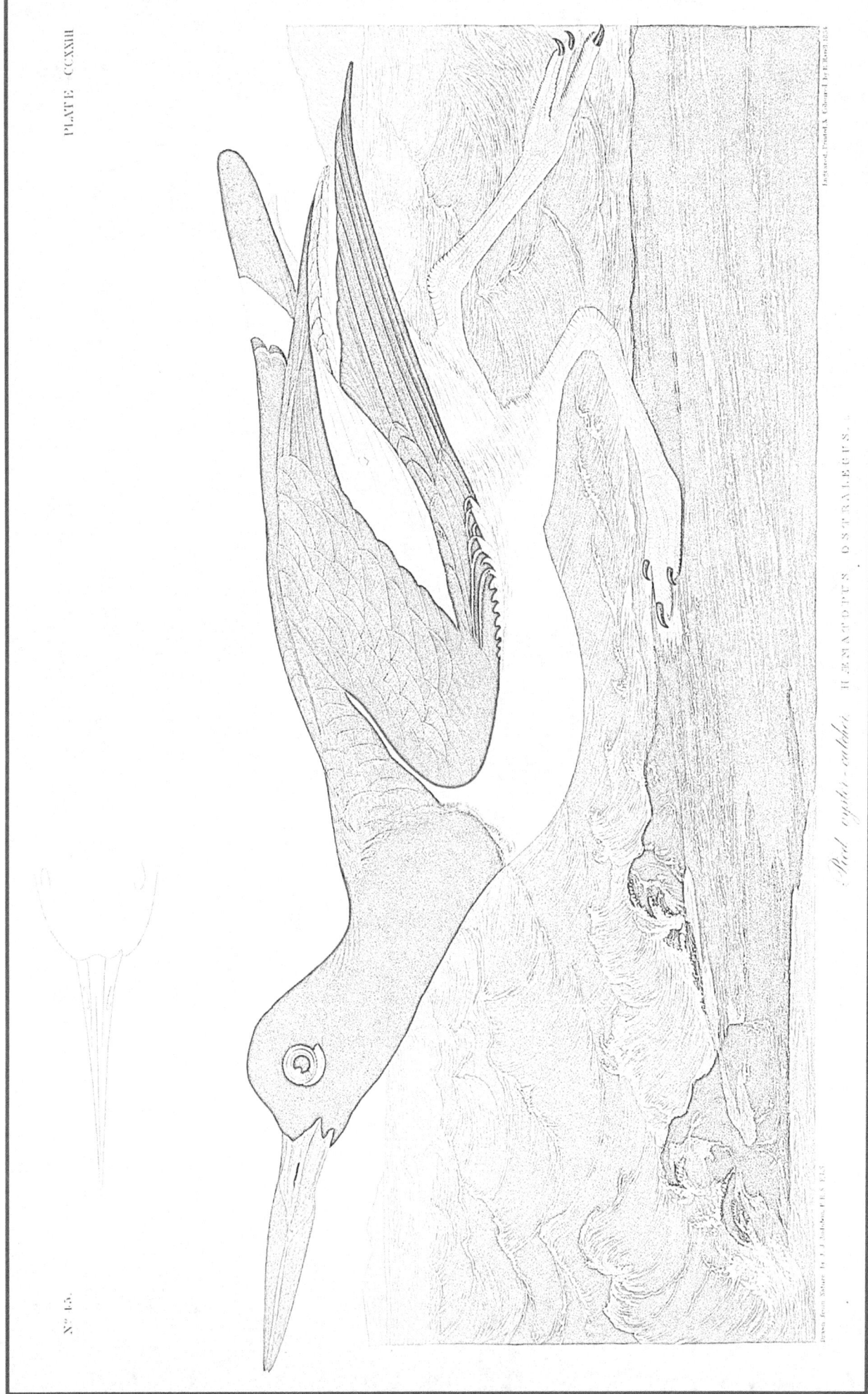

Drawn from Nature by J.J. Audubon. F.R.S.E.

Pied oyster-catcher. HÆMATOPUS OSTRALEGUS.

Engraved, Printed & Coloured by R. Havell 1834.

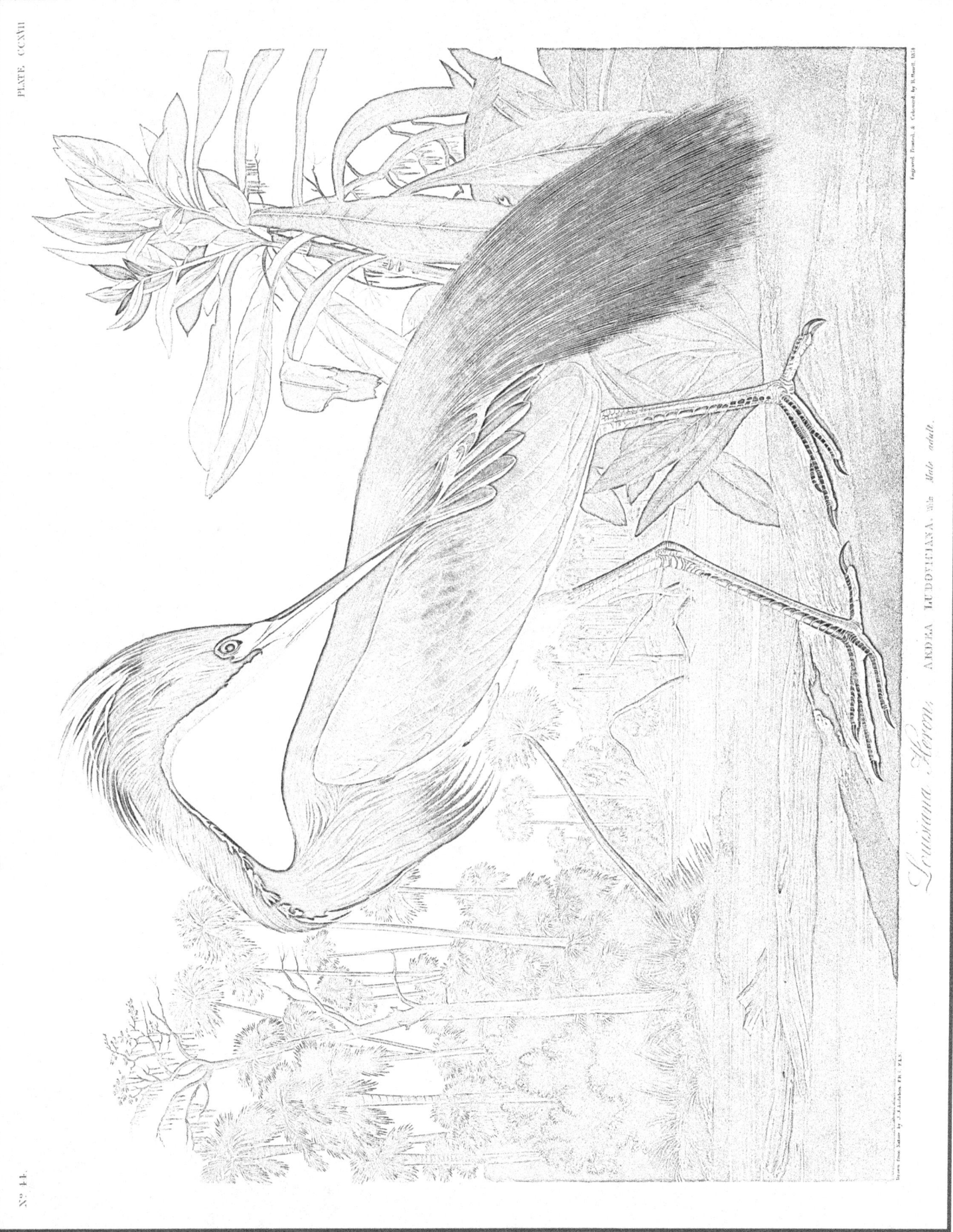

PLATE CCXVII

Louisiana Heron. ARDEA LUDOVICIANA. *Wils.* Male adult.

PLATE CCXVI.

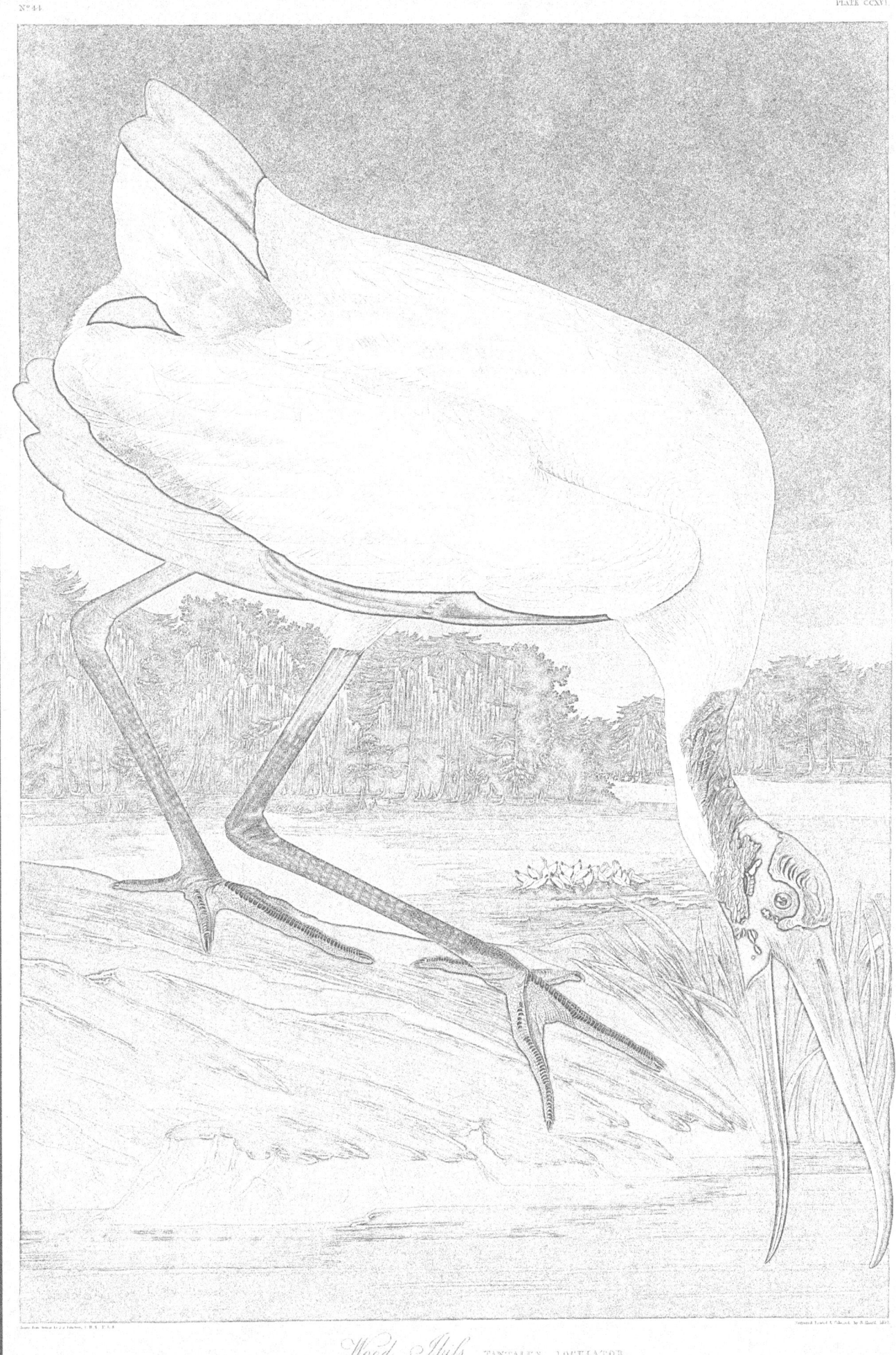

Wood Ibis TANTALUS LOCULATOR.

PLATE CCLXI

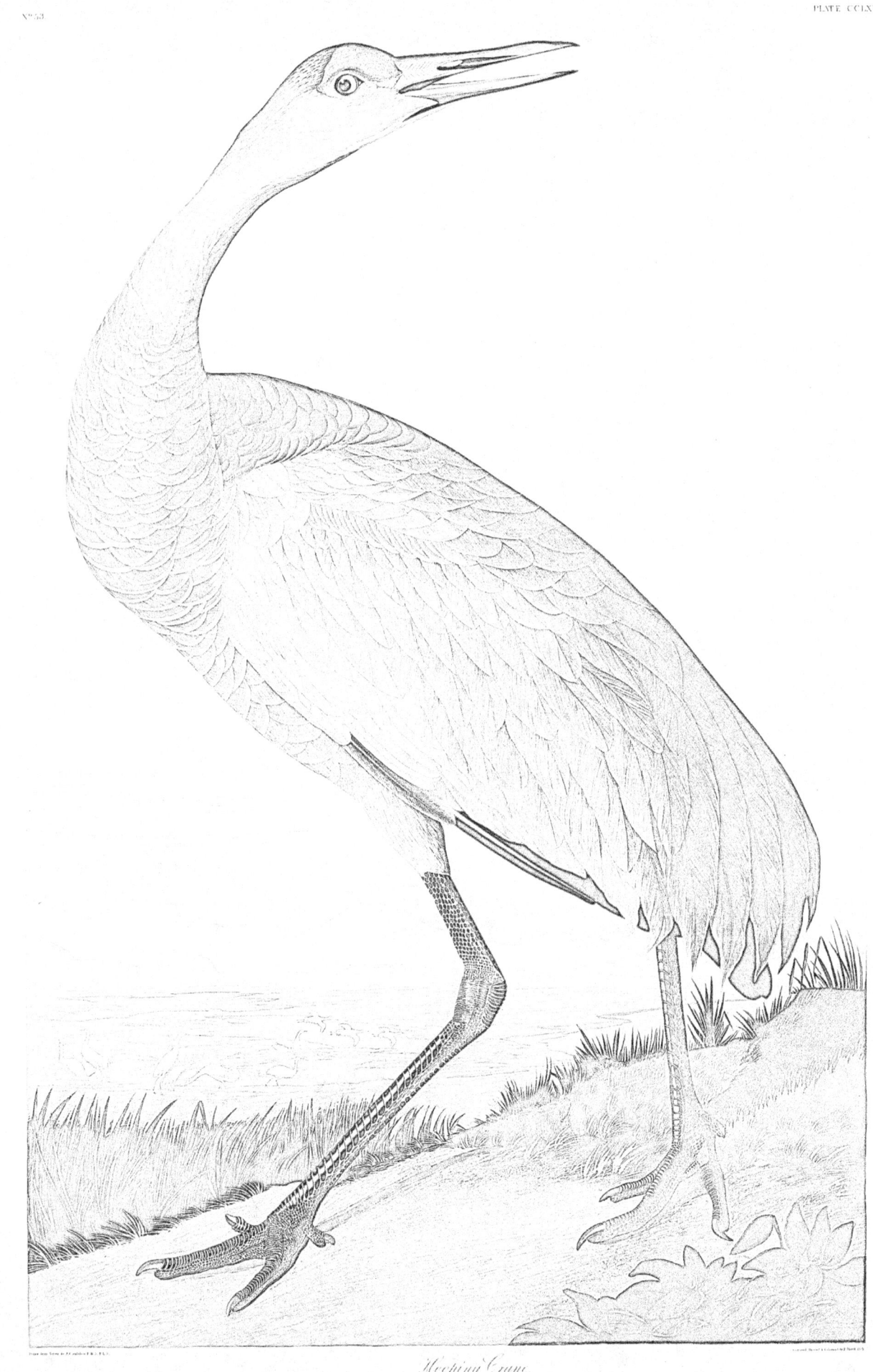

Whooping Crane
GRUS AMERICANA.
Young.

PLATE.CII.

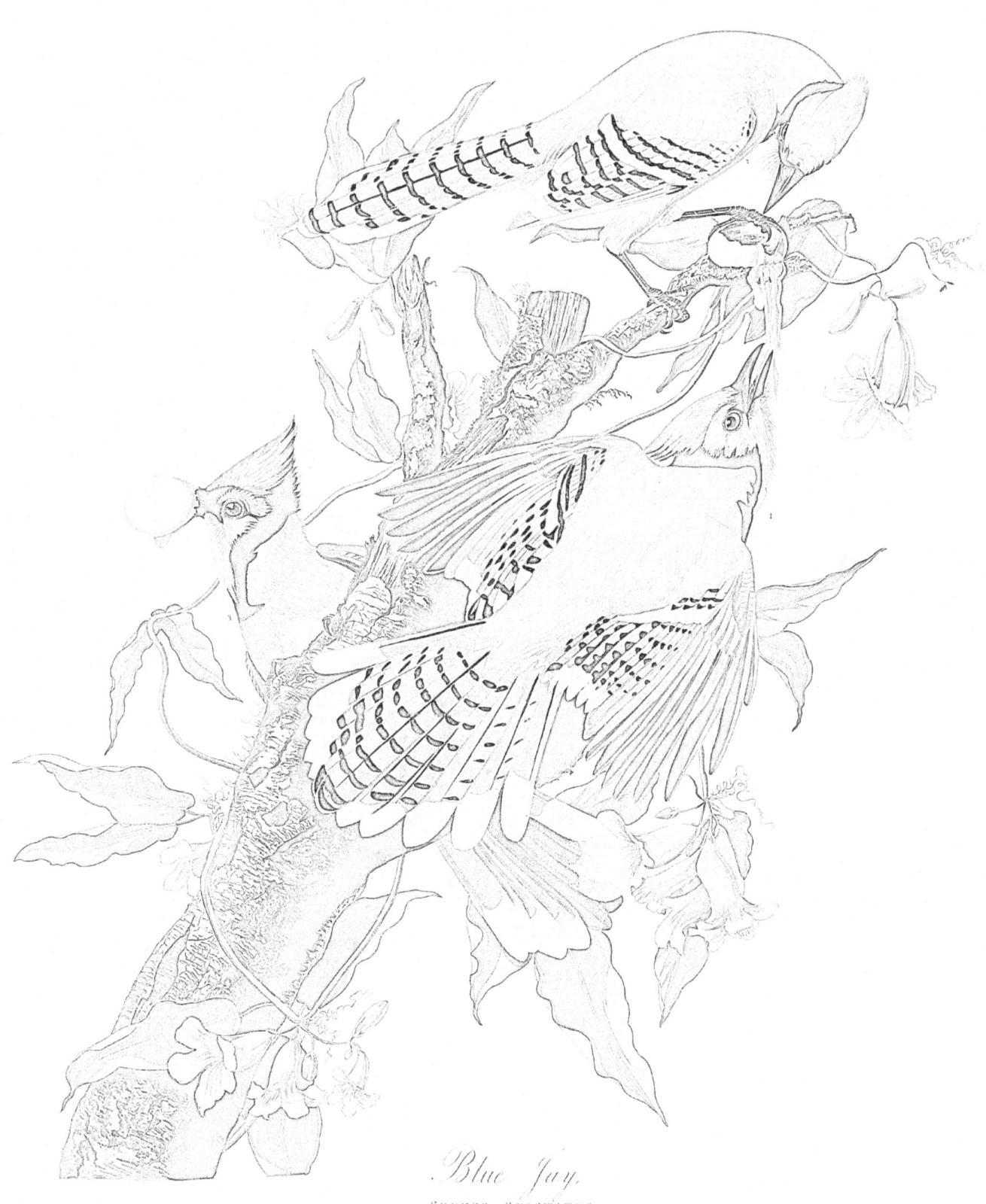

Blue Jay,
CORVUS CRISTATUS,
Male 1. Female 2.3.

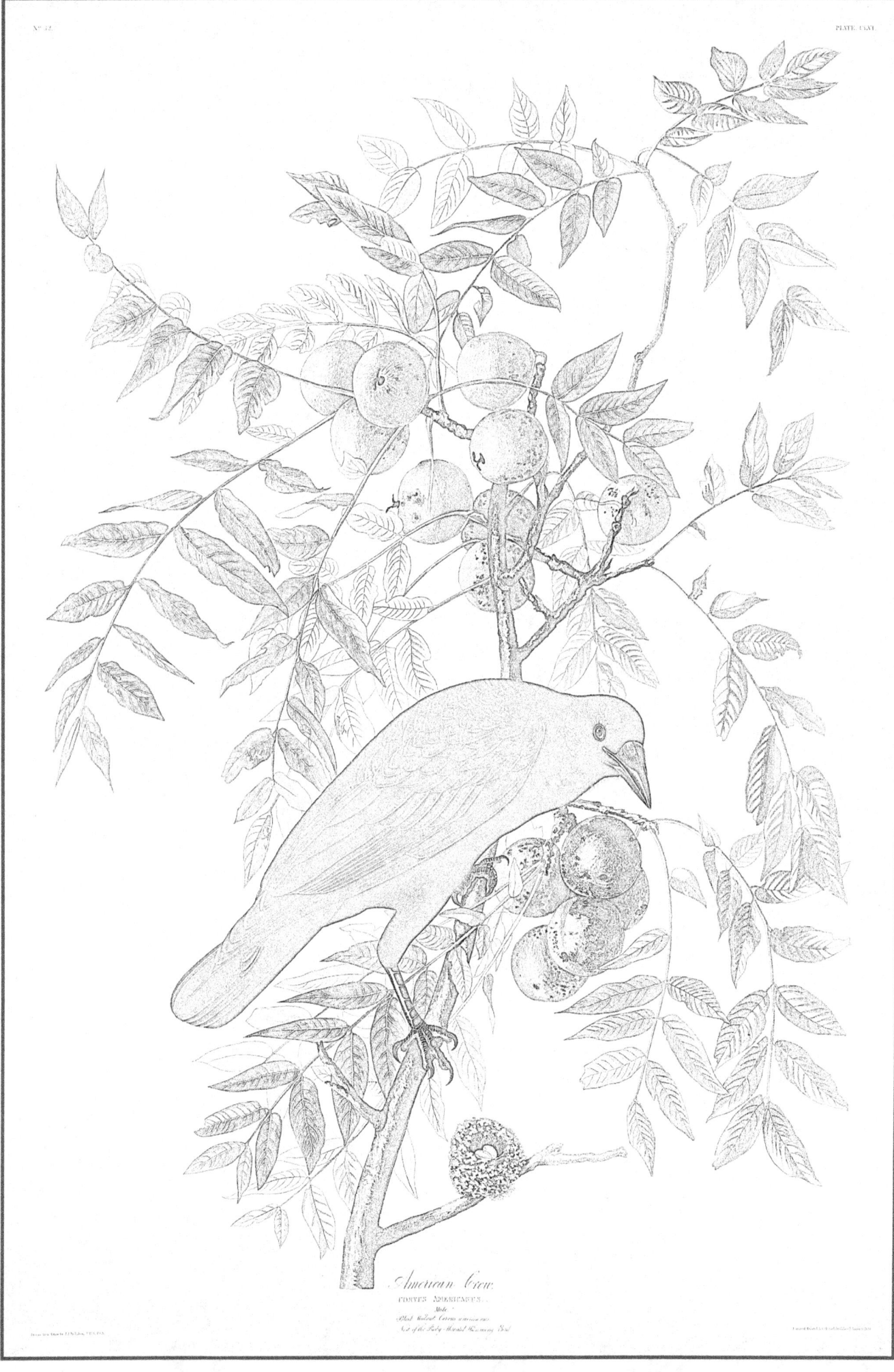

American Crow.
CORVUS AMERICANUS.
Male.
Black Walnut Corvus americanus.
Nest of the Ruby throated Humming Bird

PLATE CCCLIX.

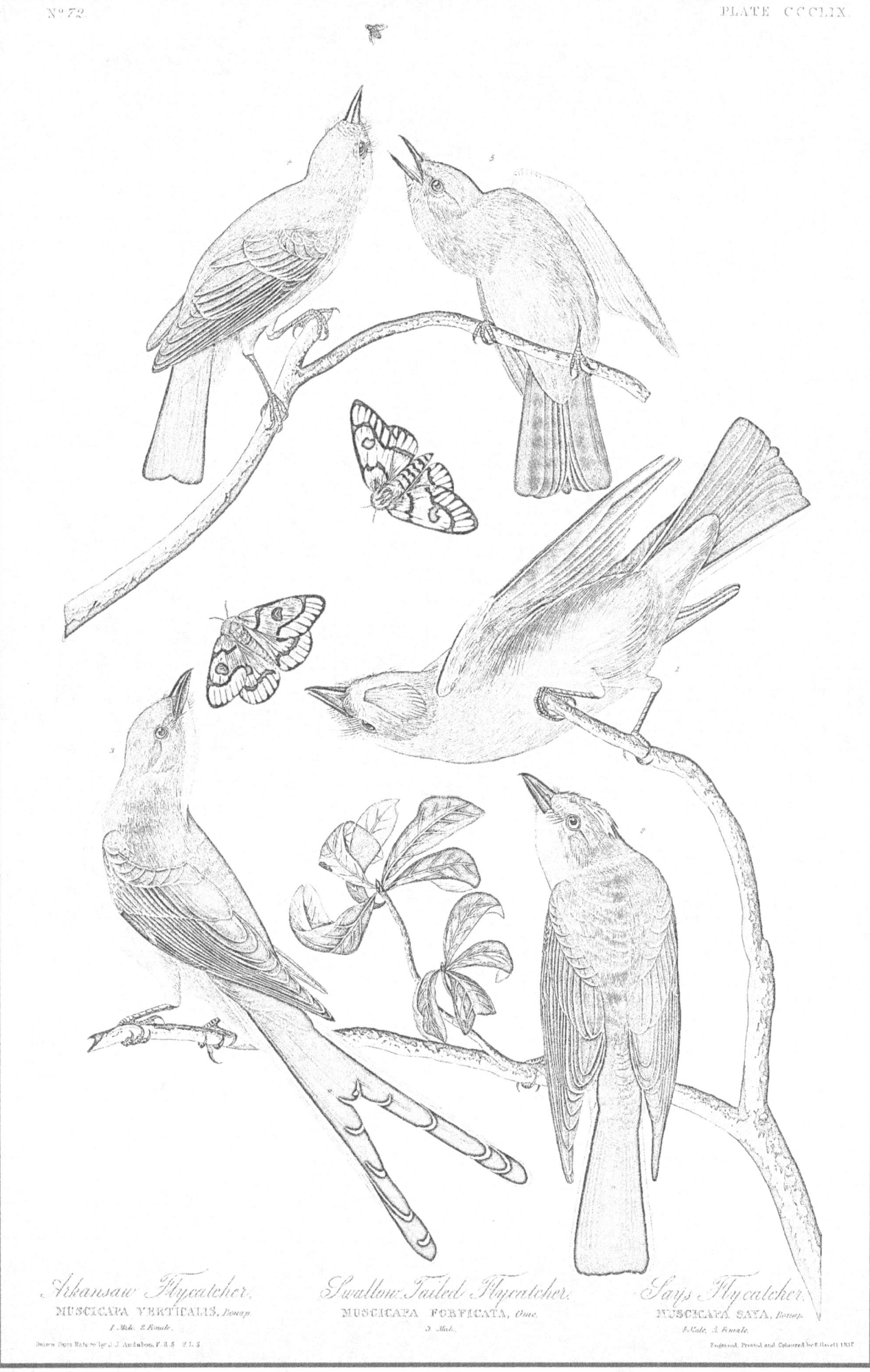

Arkansaw Flycatcher.
MUSCICAPA VERTICALIS, *Bonap.*
1 Male. 2 Female.

Swallow Tailed Flycatcher.
MUSCICAPA FORFICATA, *Gme.*
3 Male.

Says Flycatcher.
MUSCICAPA SAYA, *Bonap.*
4 Male. 5 Female.

PLATE CCLXIV

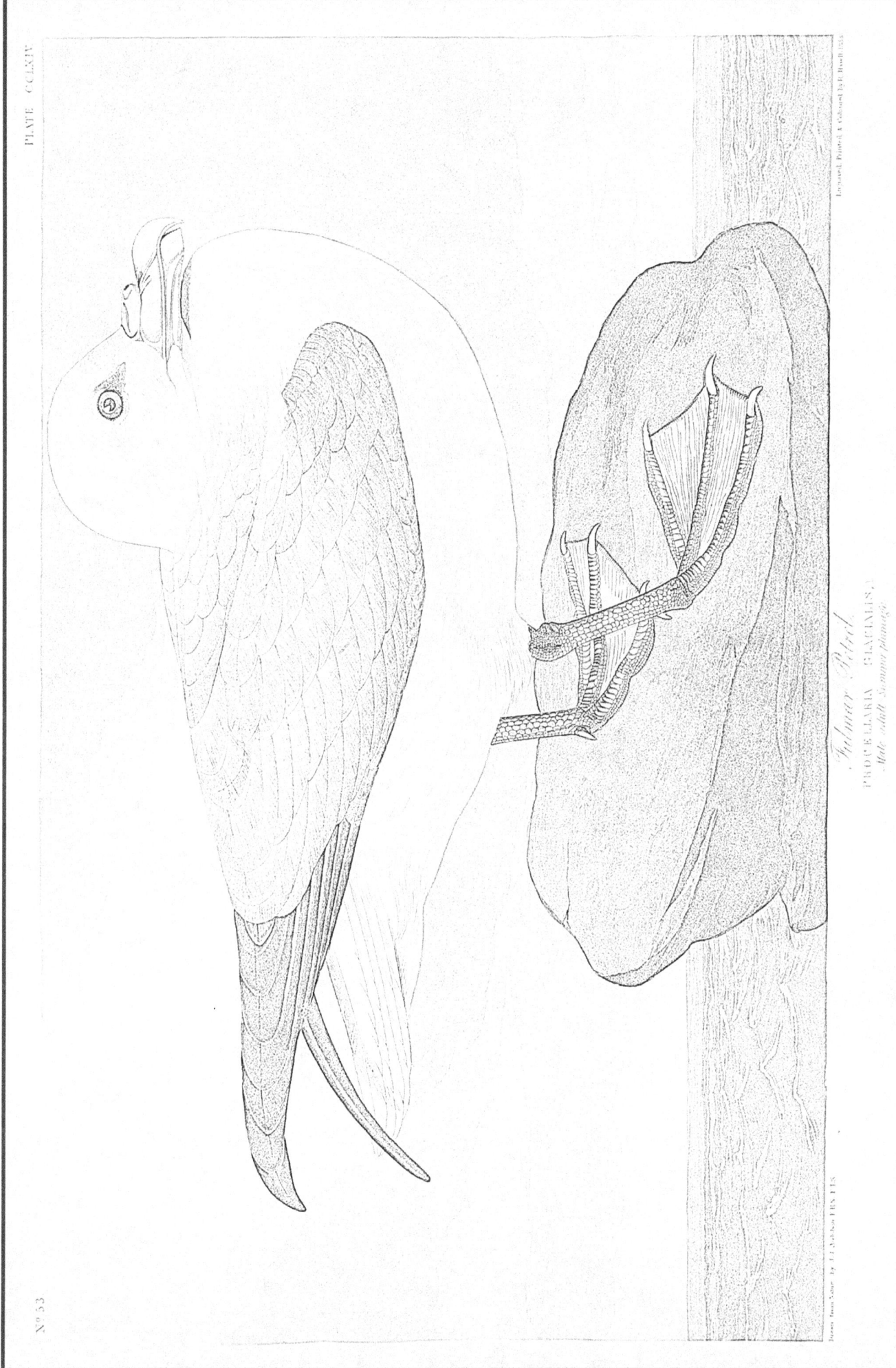

Fulmar Petrel.
PROCELLARIA GLACIALIS.
Male adult Summer plumage

PLATE CCLXIII.

N° 53.

Pigmy Curlew
TRINGA SUBARQUATA. *Temm.*
Adult. Male 1. Young 2.

Drawn from Nature by J.J.Audubon, F.R.S. F.L.S.

Engraved, Printed & Coloured by R. Havell 1833.

PLATE 96.

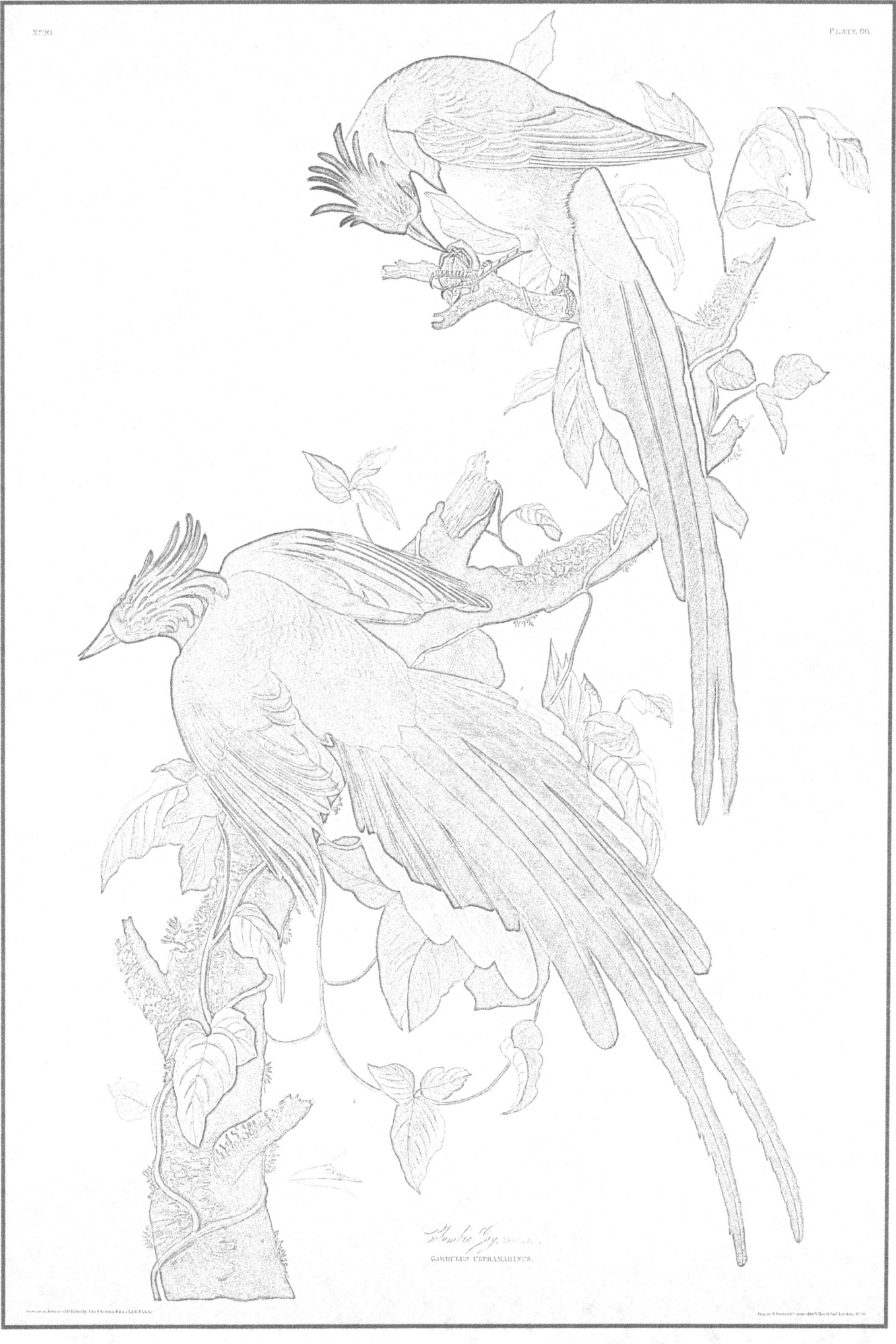

Columbia Jay.

GARRULUS ULTRAMARINUS.

PLATE CCXXII

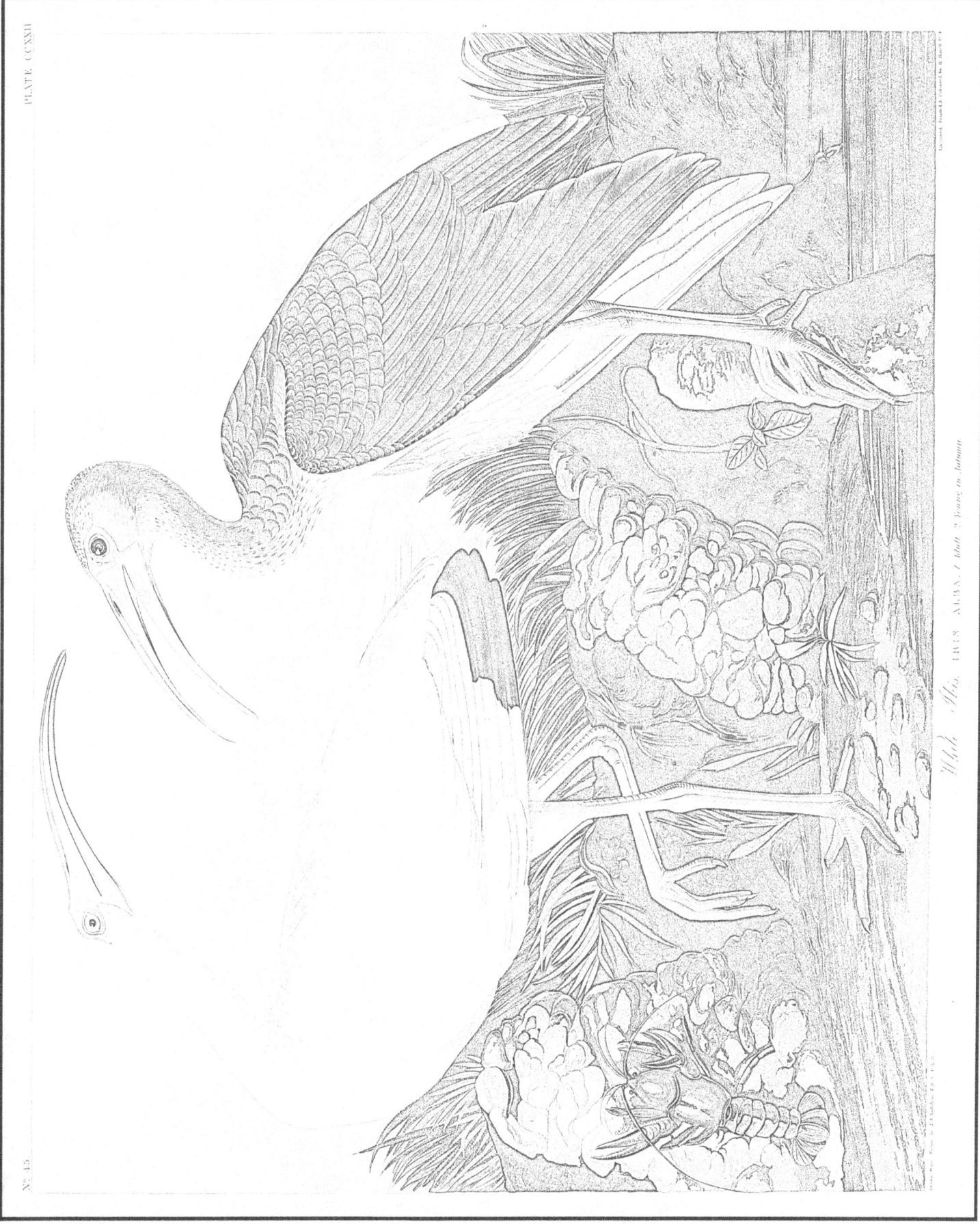

White Ibis. IBIS ALBA. / Male. 2 Years in Autumn

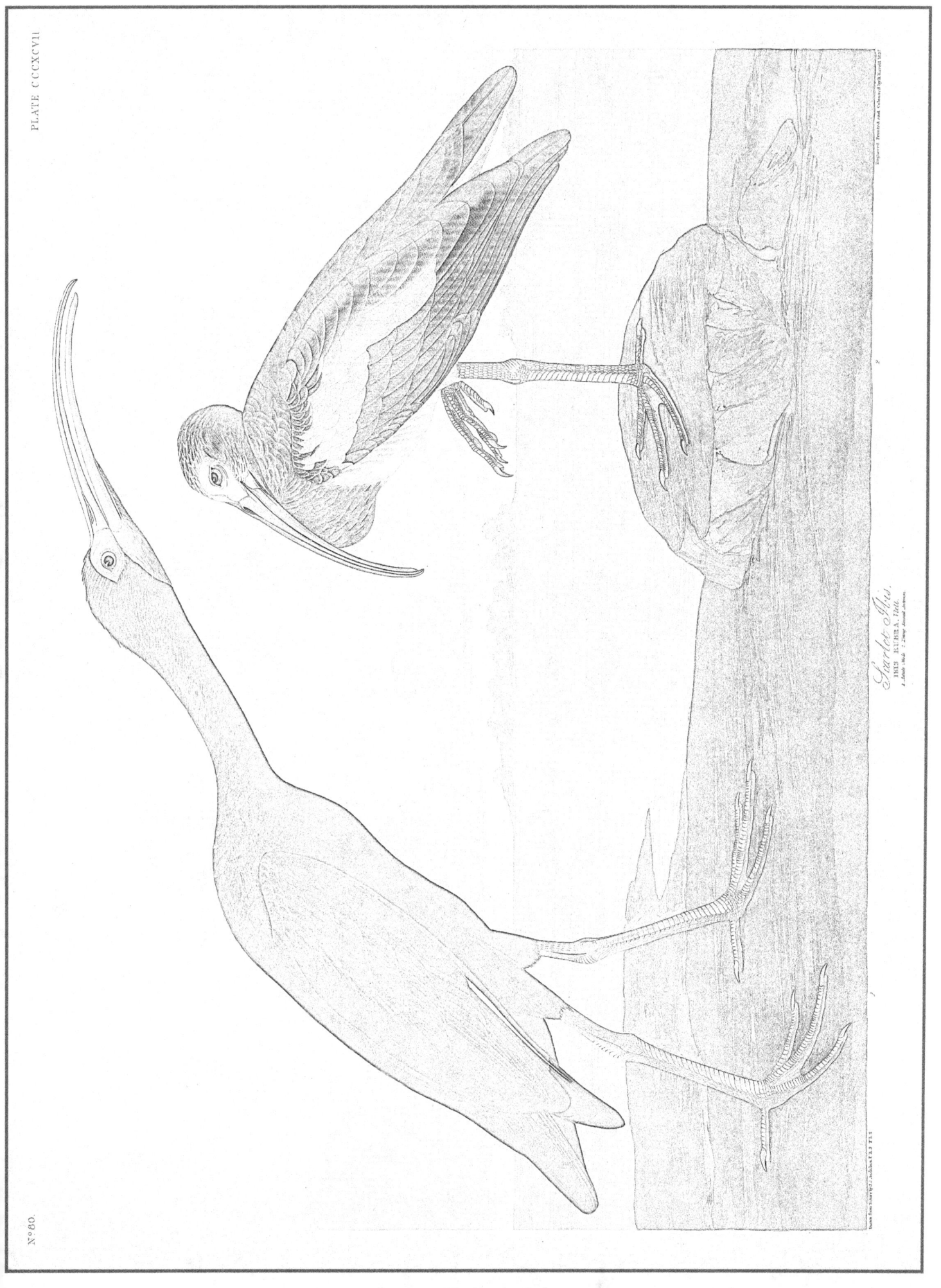

PLATE CCCXCVII

Scarlet Ibis.

PLATE CCCX

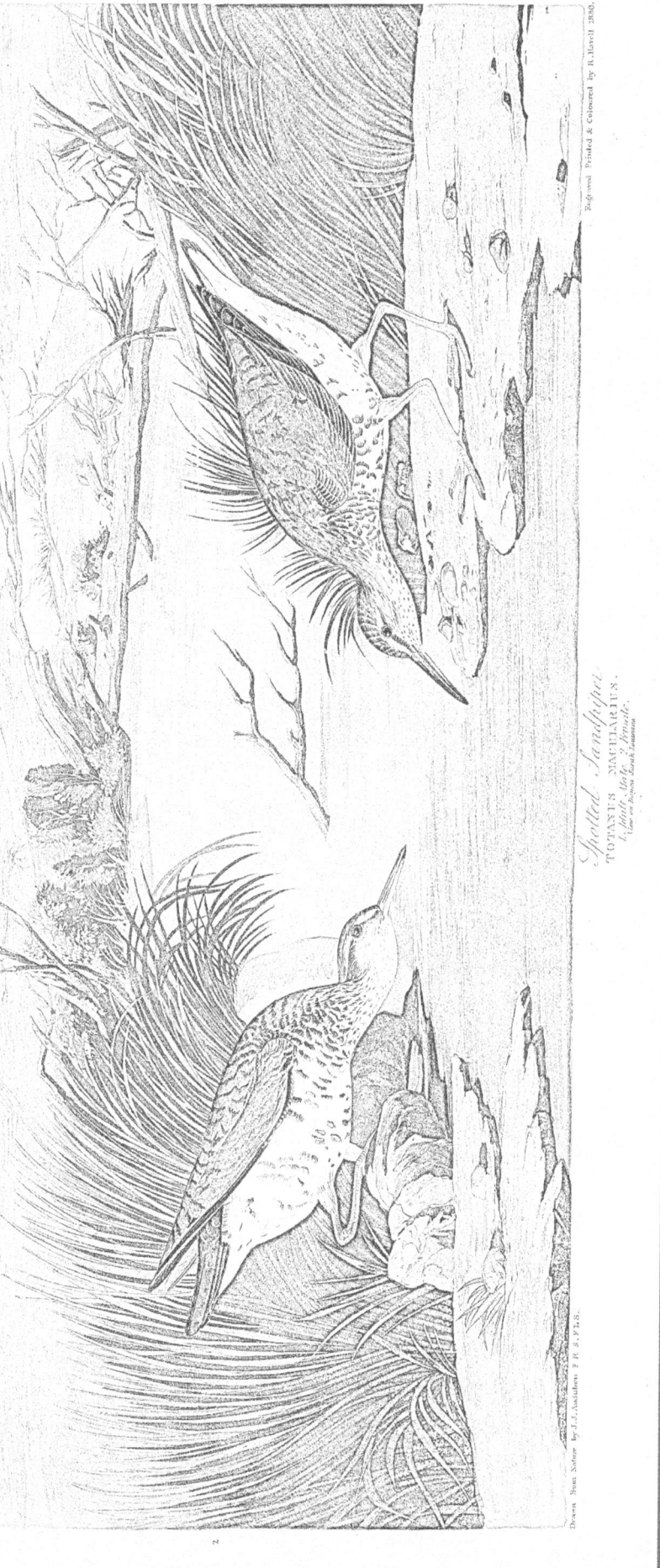

Spotted Sandpiper
TOTANUS MACULARIUS.
1. Adult Male. 2. Female.
View on Bayou Sarah, Louisiana.

PLATE CCCXXXVI

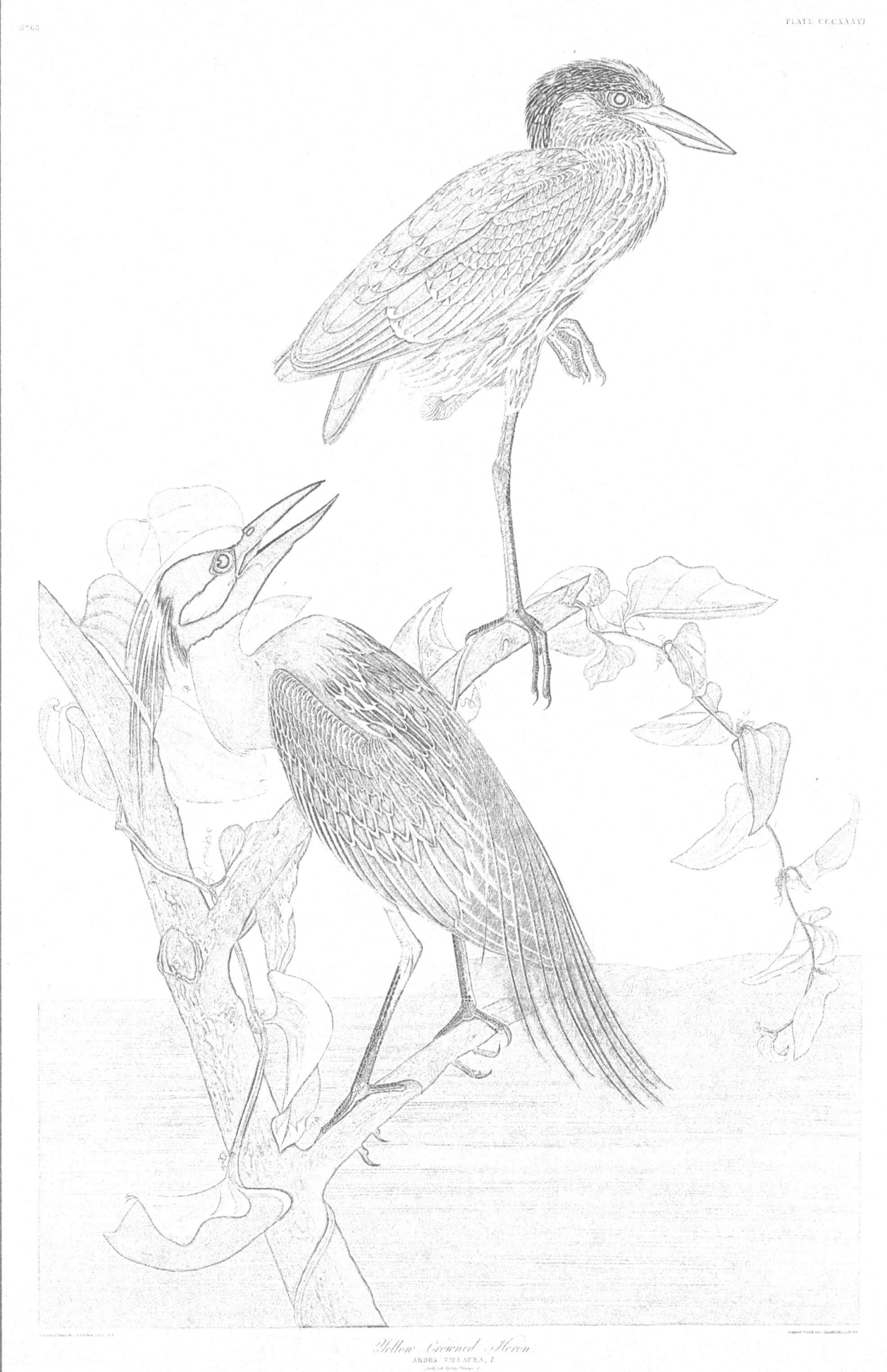

Yellow Crowned Heron.
ARDEA VIOLACEA, L.

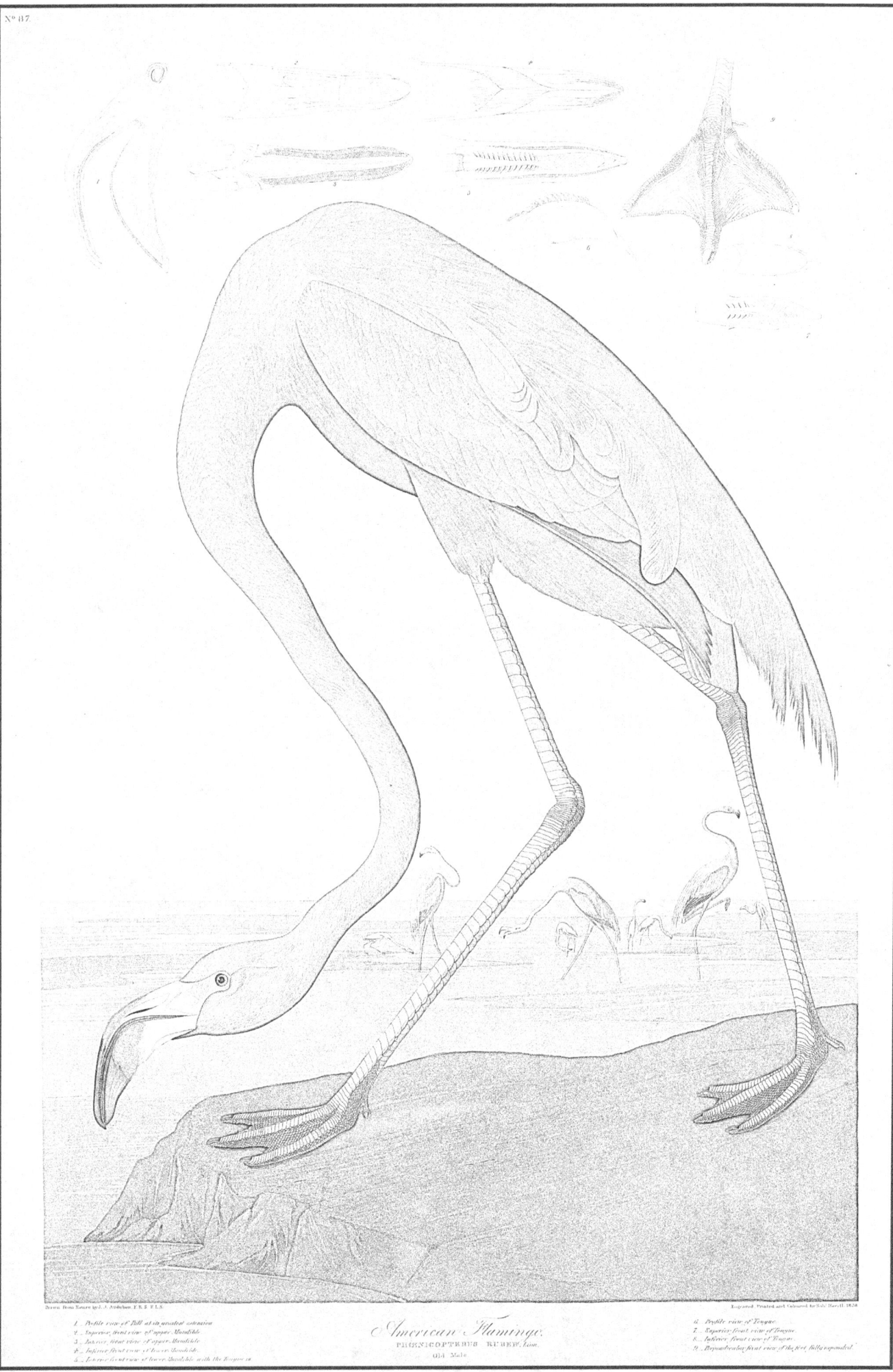

American Flamingo.
PHŒNICOPTERUS RUBER, *Linn.*
Old Male.

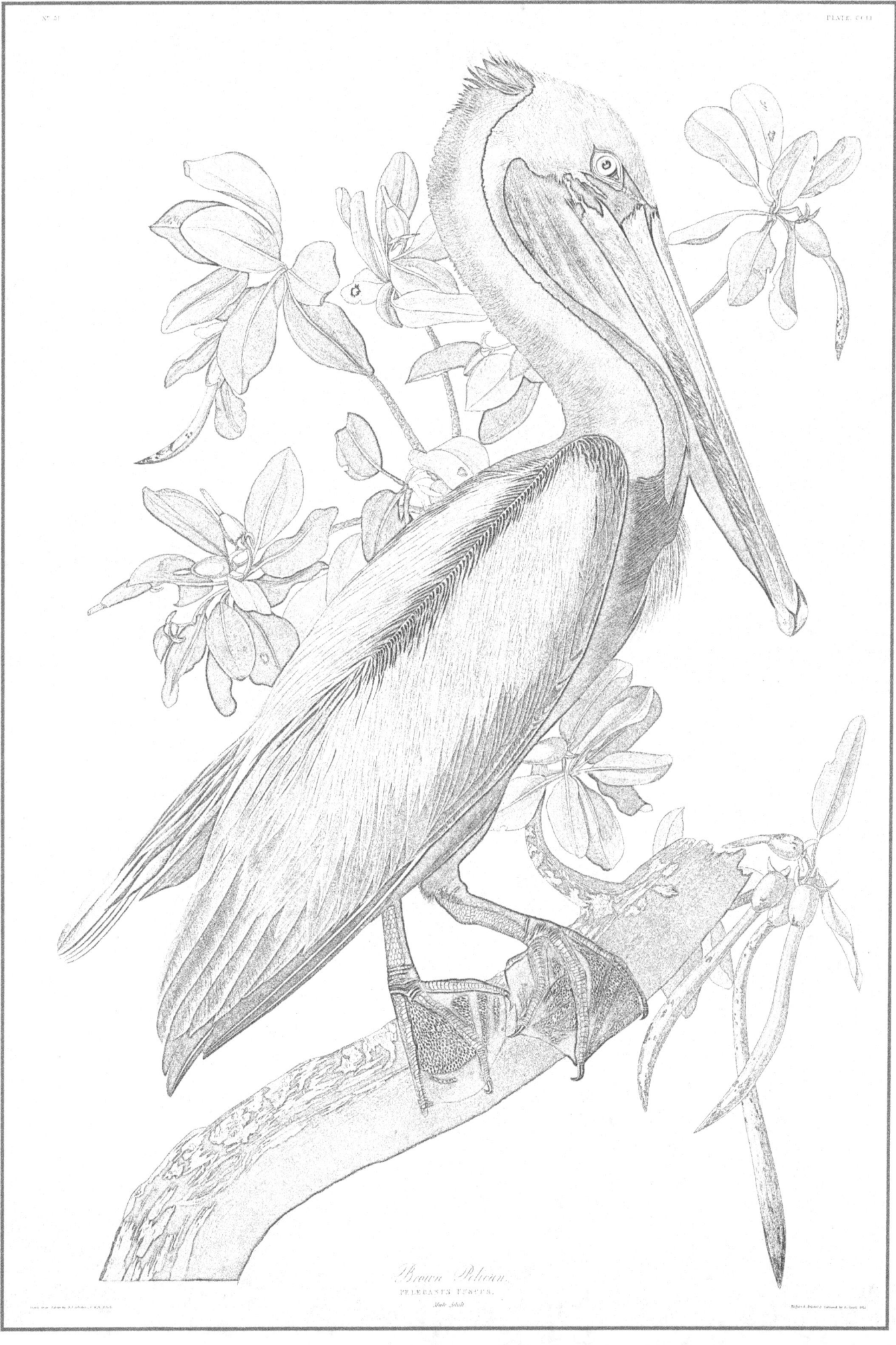

Brown Pelican.
PELECANUS FUSCUS.
Male Adult.

PLATE CCCCXXVII

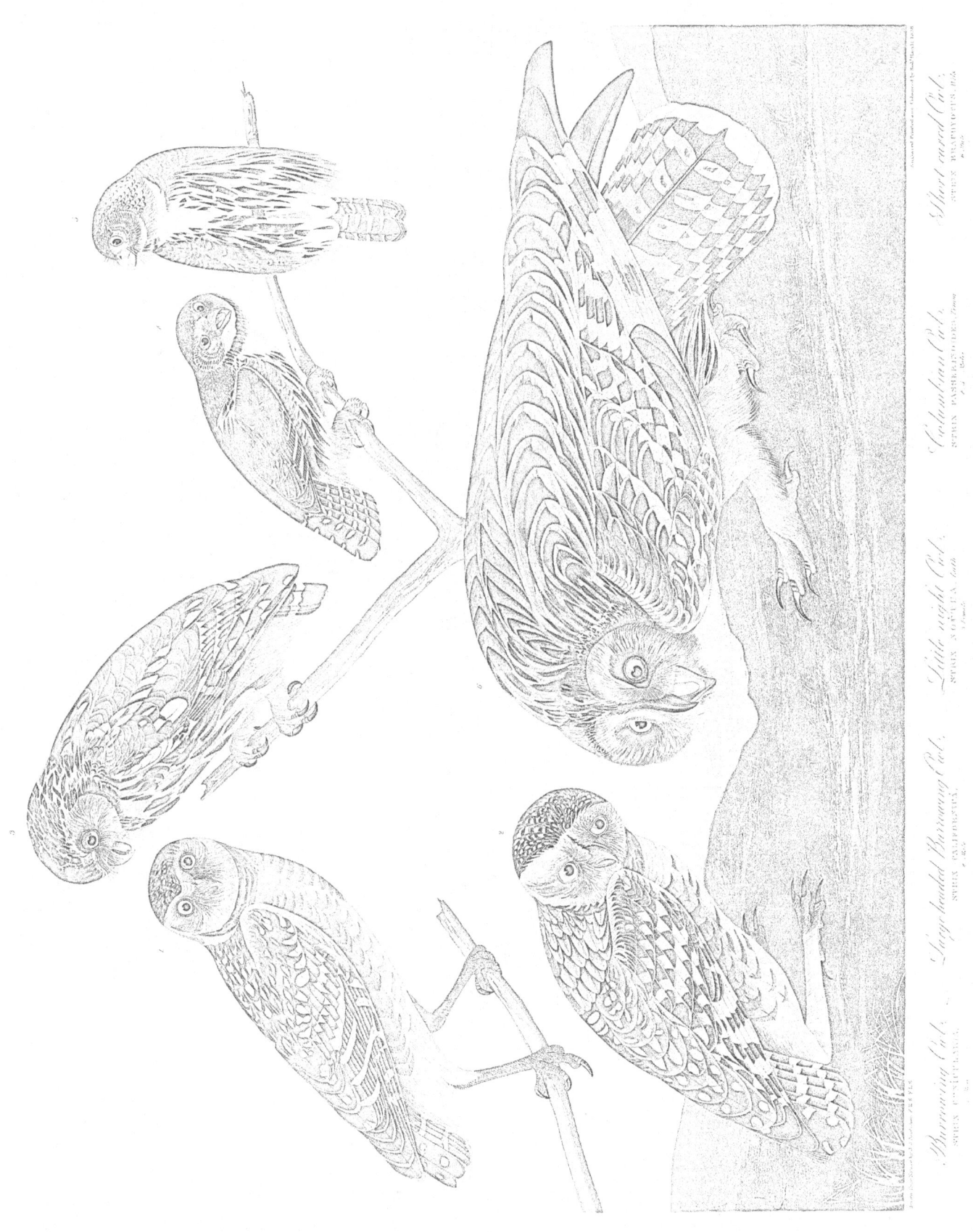

Burrowing Owl.   Large-headed Burrowing Owl.   Little night Owl.   Columbian Owl.   Short eared Owl.

PLATE CCLXIX

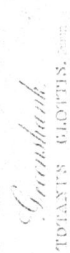

Greenshank.
TOTANUS GLOTTIS, Linn.
View of St Augustine & Savannah. Adult Male.

Drawn from Nature by J.J. Audubon, FRS FLS

Engraved, Printed & Coloured by R. Havell 1833.

PLATE CCCXCII

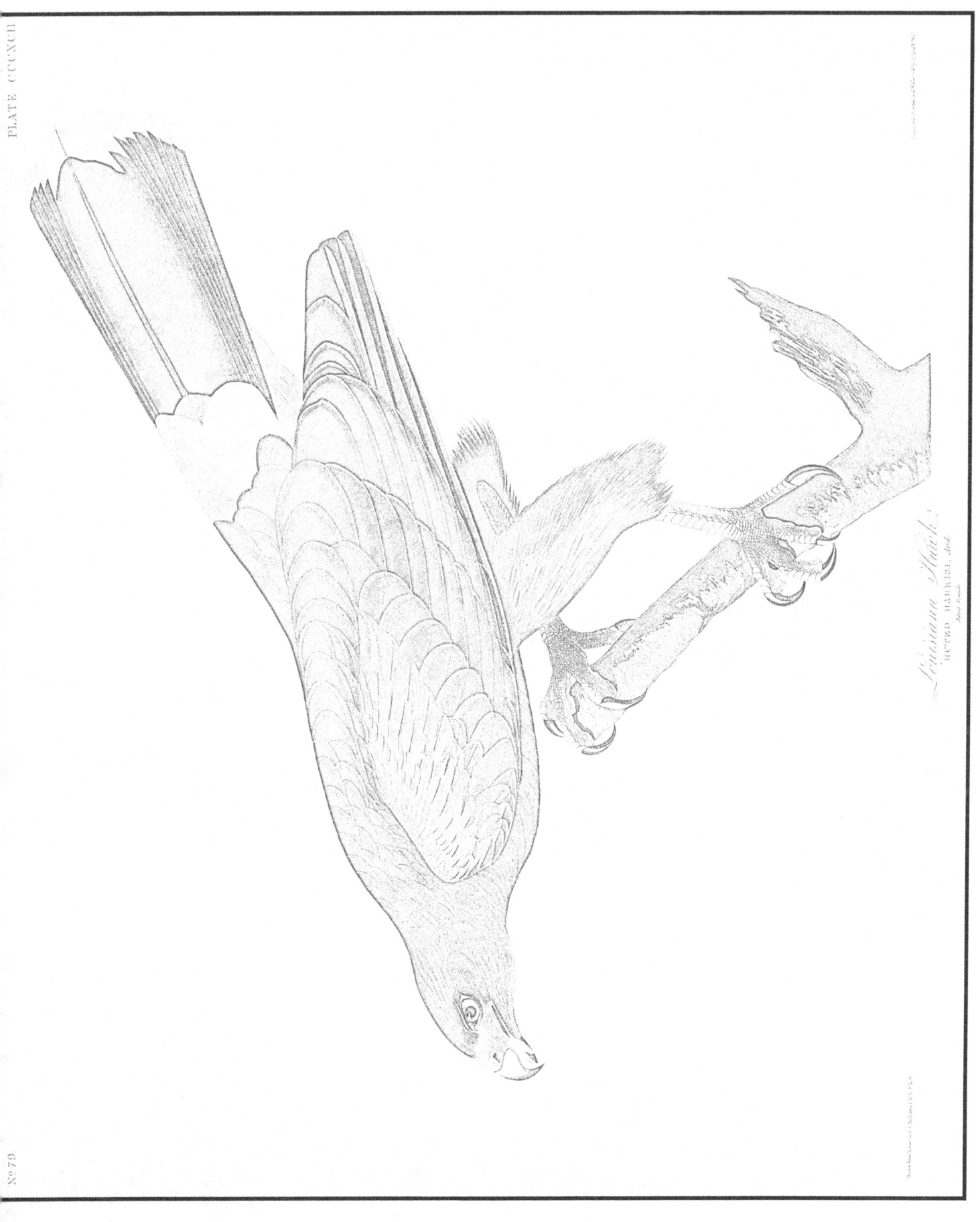

Louisiana Hawk.
BUTEO HARRISI, Aud.
Adult Female.

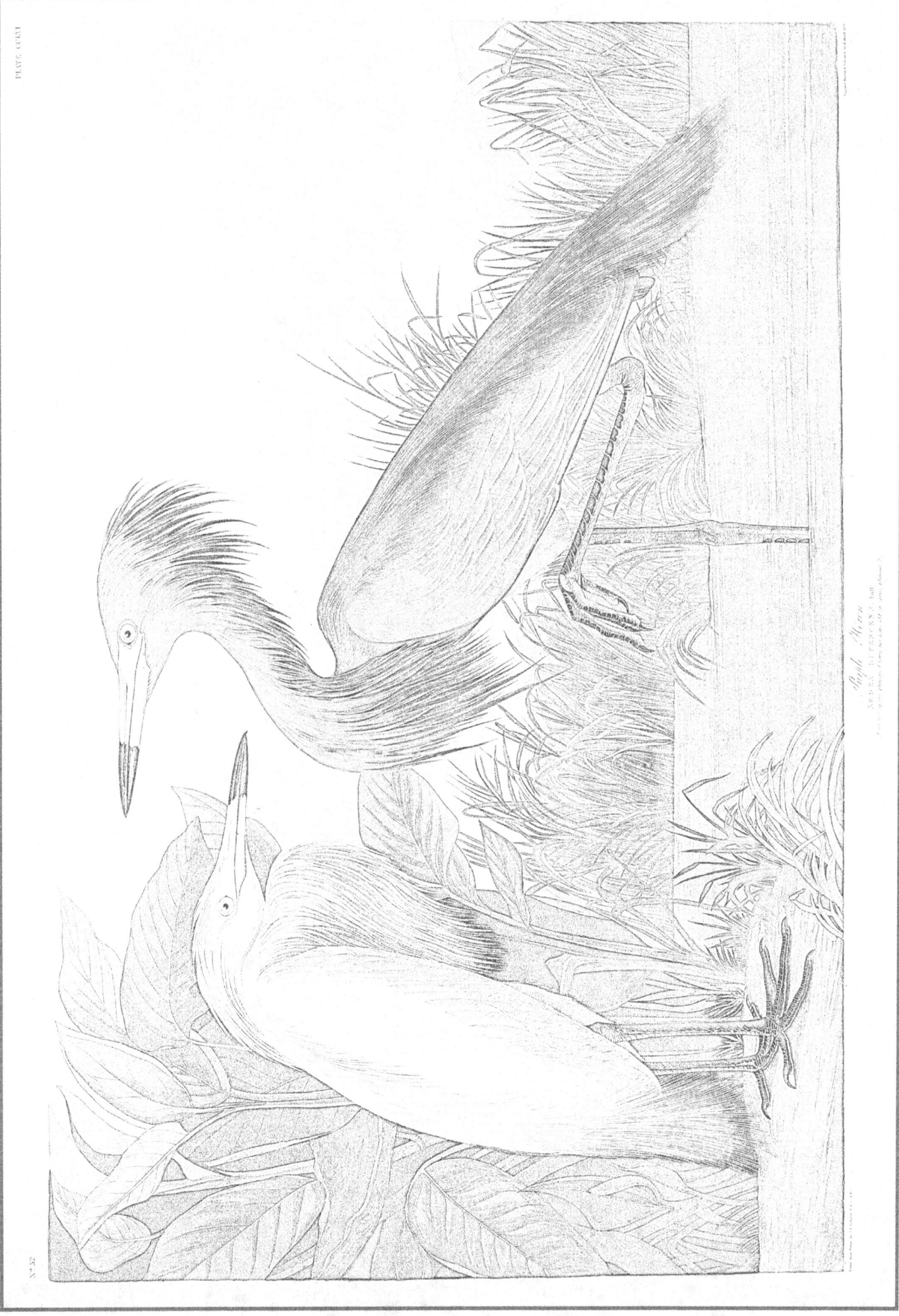

PLATE CCLXXXIX

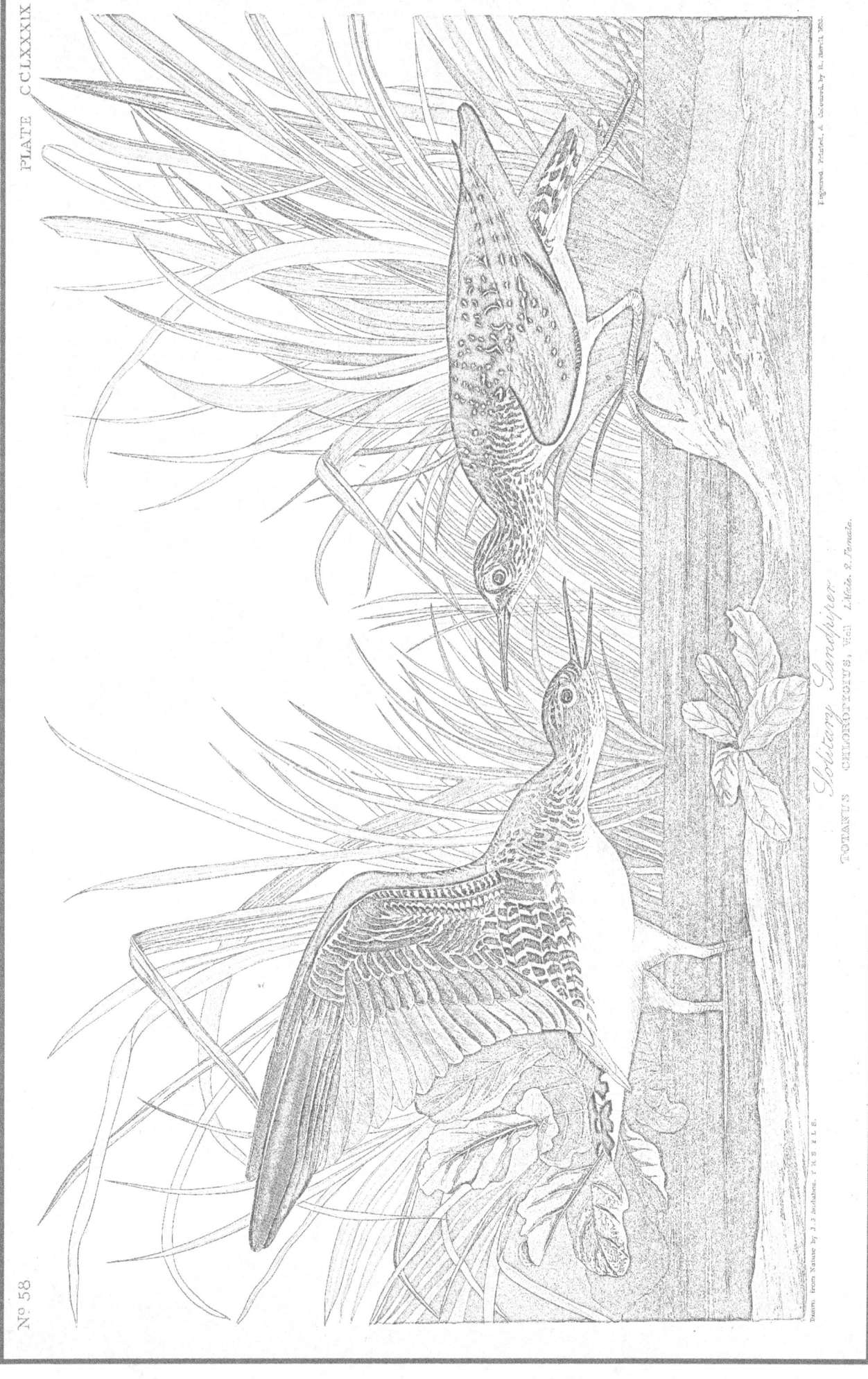

Drawn from Nature by J.J.Audubon. F.R.S.F.L.S.

Engraved Printed, & Coloured by R. Havell 1835.

Solitary Sandpiper

TOTANUS CHLOROPYGIUS, Vieill. 1.Male. 2.Female.

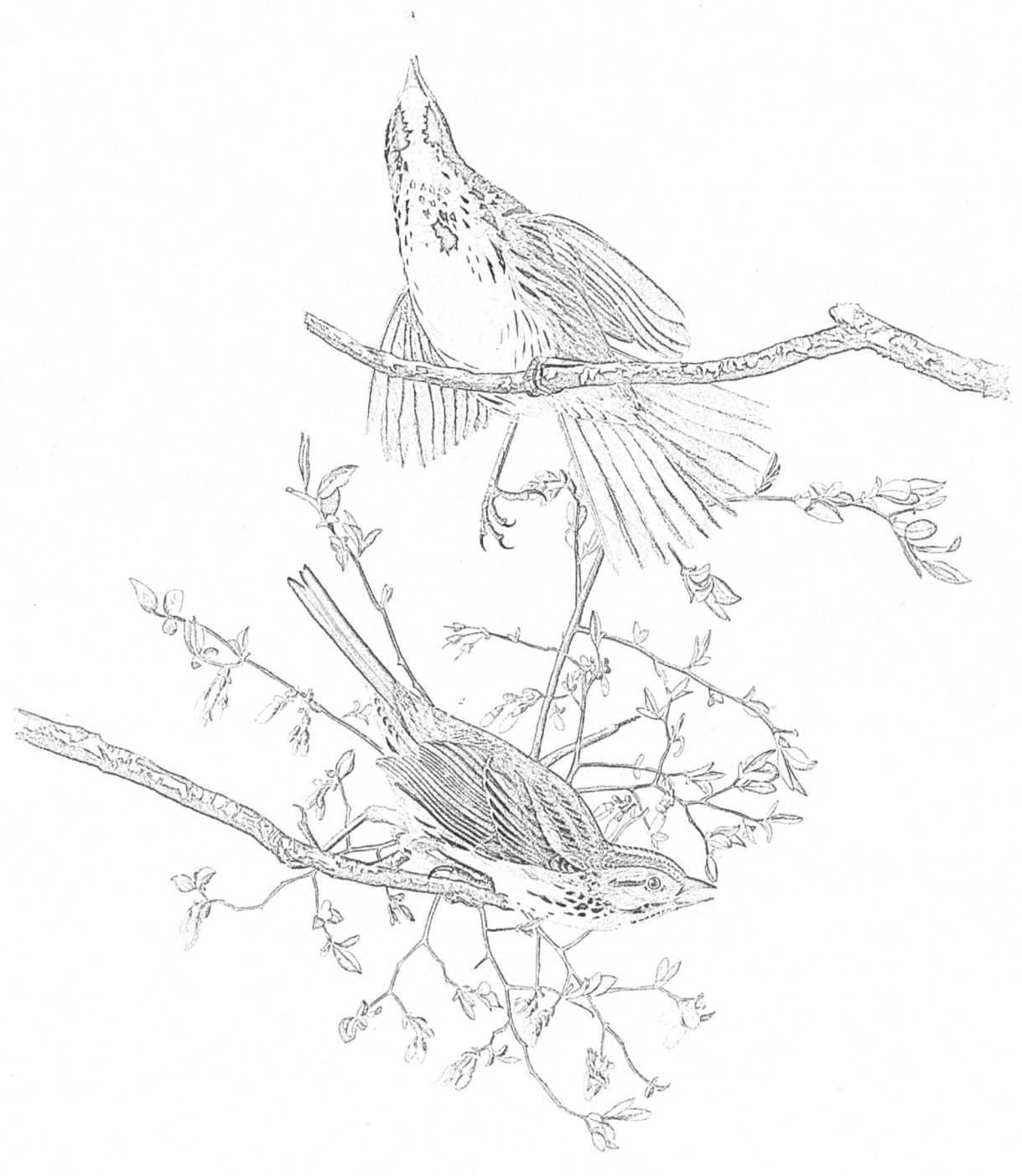

Song Sparrow. Male 1. F. 2.

FRINGILLA MELODIA.

Plant Vulgo. Wortle Berry.

Drawn from Nature and Published by John J. Audubon, F.R.S.E. M.W.S.   Engraved, Printed & Coloured by R. Havell & Son, London.

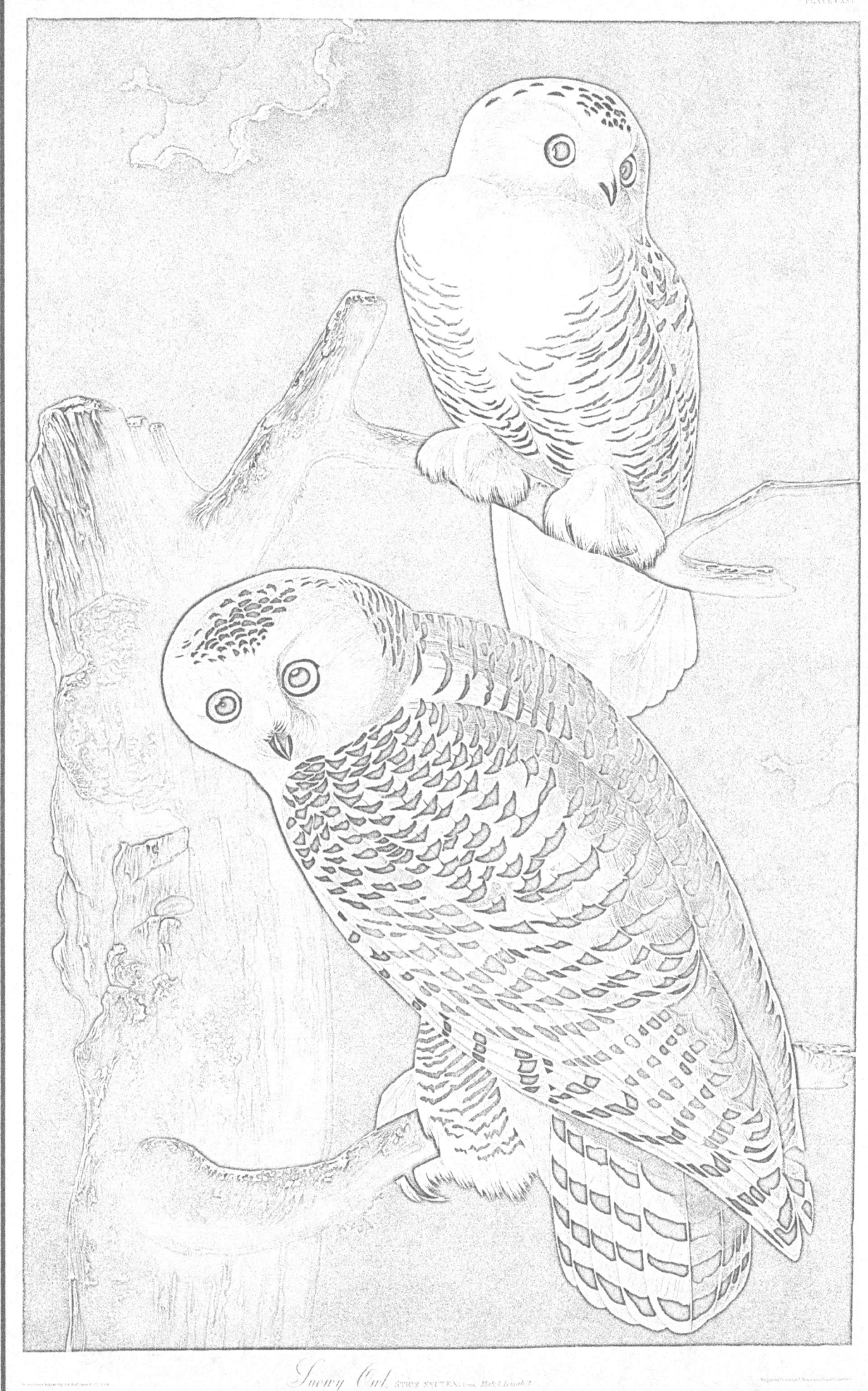

PLATE CXXI

Snowy Owl, STRIX NYCTEA, *Linn. Male & Female.*